How to Fly

poems by

Kerri Davidson

Finishing Line Press
Georgetown, Kentucky

How to Fly

Copyright © 2018 by Kerri Davidson
ISBN 978-1-63534-516-2 First Edition
All rights reserved under International and Pan-American Copyright Conventions. No part of this book may be reproduced in any manner whatsoever without written permission from the publisher, except in the case of brief quotations embodied in critical articles and reviews.

ACKNOWLEDGMENTS

"This Moment" and "Beginnings" were published by Nostalgia Press in the *Heart 12* Anthology.

Huge thanks to Dan White, the amazing artist who created the beautiful cover for this book; to Chrissy Rivela, who has encouraged me every step of the way, and to Grant Chang, who lives his dreams and inspires me to do the same.

I'd also like to thank the ladies in my writing group at Girls Write Now, who made me feel like publishing a book was a reachable dream.

And a big thanks to you, reader, for buying my paper airplane. Now let's fly….

Publisher: Leah Maines
Editor: Christen Kincaid
Cover Art and Design: Dan White. ©2017, www.danwhitedraws.com
Author Photo: Sean Turi, http://seanturi.com/

Printed in the USA on acid-free paper.
Order online: www.finishinglinepress.com
also available on amazon.com

Author inquiries and mail orders:
Finishing Line Press
P. O. Box 1626
Georgetown, Kentucky 40324
U. S. A.

Table of Contents

Something to Light Our Way 1

How to Fly 3

God 4

Beginnings 5

Audition 7

At 4am 9

Through Walls 10

When It Fell 11

The Postcard 13

Watercolor 15

Waves 17

Stuck 18

Stump 19

of brick and birds and that which I cannot see 21

Dandelion Picking 23

October Nights 24

Throwing Punches 26

This Moment 28

What Was Lost 29

This book is dedicated to my mom, Jane; dad, Wally; and sister, Kris. I cannot imagine where I would be without their unfathomable love and support. They held me close and then let me fly.

Something to Light Our Way

Summer evening dims the yard

The birds have gone home to their nests
Carefully created by entwining the compost of nature and man

Small creatures come out:
We children,
And the lightning bugs—
The small glowing points of light
That occasionally winked at us

It was their secret sign
And we ran to catch them
To hold something so bright—
Our hands glowed orange from their beams

They lit our dark world

We stored them in boxes

They died the next day,
The light too delicate to be in captivity

Just like our own quivering luminescence
As we aged into teens

Our secret plea was the same—

Find us

Love us

Set us free

How to Fly

This page is my paper ticket

somehow it will escape

I'll fly with it

First class on a paper airplane

How to Fly

This page is my paper ticket
somehow it will escape—
I'll fly with it
first class on a paper airplane

it's what I dreamed of while working in the warehouse years ago
the one thing we all shared—
the want of a way out

hopes fought stagnant air
crawled staleness toward an ear
the cardboard boxes we stacked
were shipped where our eyes pointed
where our feet dreamed of walking
though caught in parallel rows

august haze cleared enough to reveal
the untouchable horizon

we held our futures in fists
refused to let go
we knew who we would be
scotty wished to touch the moon
james was to direct movies
I was to go to new york city to write—
they asked me to write about them
to carry them with me on the page

we lugged regrets
as weights in our boxes
but vowed never to be stuck in the middle
in dim florescence

semis sighed opaque exhaust
we inhaled
and the sun set and rose in transparent pastels
then set and rose again

God

Ah…to be the air
under butterfly wings
lift them up
watch them fly
without ever being seen.

Beginnings

Sneaking a final breath
of broken air
I step across the gap
between the platform
and steel subway car
my first ride alone
in New York City

The train jolts to a start
following the red line I traced
on my map the night before
and check now again, to be sure

The subway map softens
ink smears in my hands
I will never find my way

A child crawls into
the molded seat next to me
his mittens dangle from his coat
he looks at the floor
but grabs my arm
small fingers grip tight for safety

We look forward now
together
rusty walls stream behind scratched sealed windows
he tightens his grip
I steady my arm
we fly through empty space.

Audition

Fingers brush light dust
off black suede shoes
cold greyed cement a solid foundation
yet sticky from dried soda spills & used gum
The suede smacks each time it leaves the floor
but when it hits a smooth patch
boy does it glide

Bright stadium lights glow
like stars granting wishes
we bask in the fluorescence
and space
so much air we can't wrap our arms around it
our bodies an echo in the vast sphere

Now, more than ever, you must search for the sun
even if all you can glimpse
is light splashing in a puddle

At 4am

Times seeps
through hungry cracks in the pavement
gaping mouth pleads for more

sharp heels dig
grasping for a solid step
as smoky bodies fill darkness
with echoes

a flash of a match briefly reveals a face
before returning to dim
confusion and amber drinks

the city whispers monotone
ashy buildings reach arms toward the sky

a bottle crash
whoop of a siren
mannequins scream through gated cages

we claw at the slippery moon

Through Walls

Pipes shriek at the shock
of hot water waking them
rushing through metallic joints
grit of iron in their mouths
their screams come to me
through walls painted thickly
every three years, a new layer of cream skin

A crash from the apartment next door
ceramic pieces shatter against hardwood floors
I pause and wait
curses reassure me—all is ok

Raised voices fight their way under my front door
two people in the hallway
yelling or laughing
distance distorts—I cannot be sure

Months ago I was awakened by pounding on the wall
the wall solidly accepting the blows
screams and foreign words penetrated
the foot of wall between my neighbor and I
I pounded back
seeking silence, a thicker wall, one quiet night
she attacked the wall harder
this barrier of cells holding her inside

Today we passed in the hall
a scarf wrapped her newly shaved head
her secret escaping through cream cloth
in her metallic eyes I remember the moment we shared
when it must have come screaming out
when humanity slipped through walls

When It Fell

and now the sky is concrete
a square slab of grey
squeezing through slits
in the blinds

your whispers slip through miles of cable
siphoned
and dripping from a perforated receiver
i hold the phone to my ear
words pour out

tears fall thick as cement from above
cracking ground that once held our weight
the indentation
is bigger than both of us

we now know what distance is—
how far it is when we're apart
how far when we're together

THE POSTCARD

THE WORDS WE EXCHANGE
ARE BLOCK-LETTERED,
CLUMSILY FORMED ON STIFF RECTANGULAR POSTCARDS—
A THESAURUS OF GENERIC GREETINGS
AT A 28¢ RATE

I TRACE YOUR LATEST WITH MY FINGER
EXHUMING YOUR TOUCH
AS THE SUN SETS IN A WAVE OF LAVENDER
ON THE FRONT OF THE CARD
WASHING OUT THE FADING BLUE SKY

NIGHT IS FALLING FASTER
THAN I CAN HOLD IT BACK

LEAVING ME ISOLATED
IN THIS DARKENING LANDSCAPE

I KNOW IT'S TIME TO TURN AROUND

STILL I FOLD THIS CARD
AND HIDE IT IN MY WORN COAT POCKET
TO HOLD SOMETHING THAT ONCE HELD YOU.

FIRST CLASS POSTAGE

The Postcard

The words we exchange
are block-lettered,
clumsily formed on stiff rectangular postcards—
a thesaurus of generic greetings
at a 34¢ rate

I trace your latest with my finger
exhuming your touch
as the sun sets in a wave of lavender
on the front of the card
washing out the fading blue sky

night is falling faster
than I can hold it back

leaving me isolated
in this darkening landscape

I know it's time to turn around

still I fold this card
and hide it in my worn coat pocket
to hold something that once held you.

Thick rain fall from the highest building
Or what is beyond
Paint me a color that stays

Watercolor

tressled train tracks form a fallen ladder
climbing horizontally
cutting a scar through paisley trees
through unbudging brick-laden towns

the past slurs by in drunken lines
sealed windows frame the years
tied to interlocking tracks
memories form an inch of silt
sticking to the glass

will this steel drop off to a vast ocean
will it let me stop
let me scratch out what was written
to follow new signs—
those of yield or stop
of dripping paint, unsealed

thick rain fall from the highest building
or what is beyond
paint me a color that stays

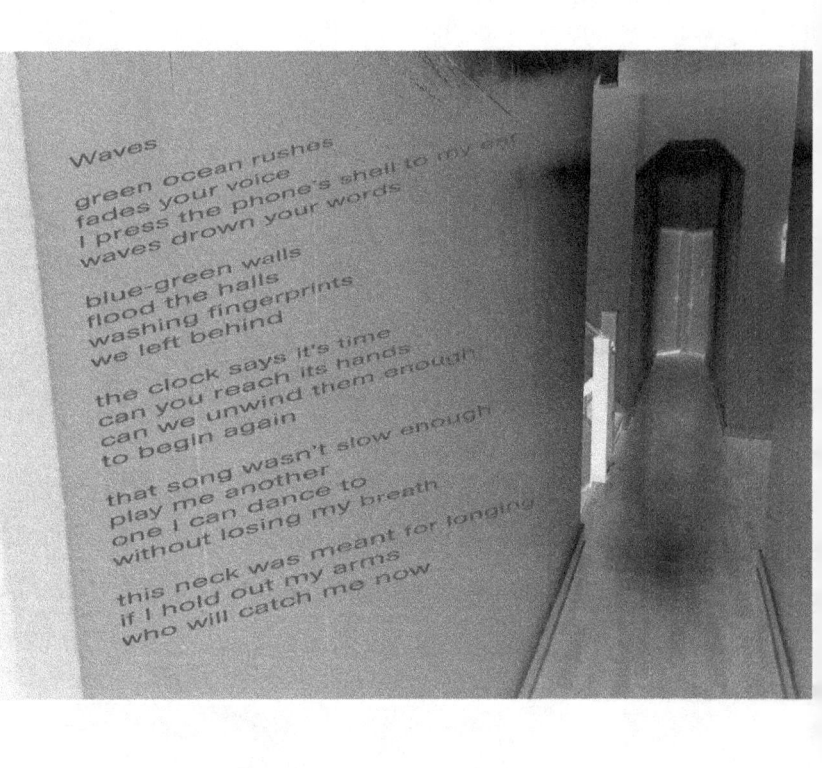

Waves

green ocean rushes
fades your voice
I press the phone's shell to my ear
waves drown your words

blue-green walls
flood the halls
washing fingerprints
we left behind

the clock says it's time
can you reach its hands
can we unwind them enough
to begin again

that song wasn't slow enough
play me another
one I can dance to
without losing my breath

this neck was meant for longing
if I hold out my arms
who will catch me now

Waves

green ocean rushes
fades your voice
I press the phone's shell to my ear
waves drown your words

blue-green walls
flood the halls
washing fingerprints
we left behind

the clock says it's time
can you reach its hands
can we unwind them enough
to begin again

that song wasn't slow enough
play me another
one I can dance to
without losing my breath

this neck was meant for longing
if I hold out my arms
who will catch me now

Stuck

rain deepens puddles
as we exit the movie
hand-in-thought

time, a discarded newspaper,
sticks to pavement in the dampness
smearing our headlines
into a foggy blur

you tilt your hat down to guard your eyes
I spin my black umbrella
so the broken part is behind me
and the front half tilts to uncover my face

we break at each puddle
to avoid diving in

bubble-wrap drops
pop on empty store windows
distorting our reflections

We walk
and try to hold back the rain

Stump

If I steal your kaleidoscope eyes
will you see me
If I run my fingers through your flyaway hair
will it look the same to you
If I hold your hand every time I close my eyes
can I hold your hand
every time I close my eyes
Can I close
my eyes
my wooden eyes
with rings of time inside
telling the story of each flood
and spark I've seen
though when they're closed
they're no longer a stump
but a tree
reaching for light

On brick and birds and that which I cannot see

Beyond transparent glass I assume is sky
stacked with mortared seams
That's my view at least, a brick wall

When I think of you I see the wall
Layers upon layers of hardened clay
And I am it—thick, unbudging

I am no bird

Birds flutter, birds fly, birds are pushed from their
nests and caught, pushed then caught
Until they need no more saving and soar to the blue
I can only assume is above
When pushed I fall
All the way down

How will I know you will not find my layered flaws
and fly
To where there is light and love and
that which I cannot see
With those not hardened, sinking from it
Those who can catch the air and let it lift them up
Those who cannot fall

of brick and birds and that which I cannot see

slouching in the sagging middle of my brown suede love seat
behind me latticed metal bars keep thugs out of my nyc apartment
beyond that I assume is sky stacked with mortared seams
that's my view at least, a brick wall

I used to have a patch of denim sky, but I tell myself this is better
the wall provides solitude, quiet

the only sounds that find me are the pet birds that fly in the ground floor apartment
so far below I cannot even see them
I just wake to their songs and am amazed
bird songs in the middle of the city

when I think of you I think of them
these neon green parakeets, mimicking, whistling
a shock of song in the dark of morning
lovebirds who sing only briefly, when I cannot predict and cannot see

when I think of you I see the brick wall
layers upon layers of pressed, hardened clay and I am it
thick, unbudging

I am no bird

birds flutter, birds fly, birds are pushed from their nests and caught,
pushed then caught, until they need no more saving and catch the air
and soar to the blue that I can only assume is above
when pushed I fall
all the way down

the lovebirds in their teen colors chatter and flip past
not seeing my chalky eyes through the latticed glass
and though I still feel the gentleness of your light touch on my brown suede coat
the one that made me blush bricks
though I wish I'd lifted my face to you—I am not used to looking up

how will I know you will not find my rocky flaws and fly
to where there is light and life and love and that which I cannot see
with those not hardened sinking from it
those who can catch the air and let it lift them up
those who cannot fall

Dandelion Picking

I spent years
wishing I could fly away
blowing white dandelion puffs
across far-reaching fields
sending seeds in my place
to search for homes in the wind

where would I find them now
those blown away wishes

maybe they're growing into mini-yellow sunbursts
shooting rays in fields and playgrounds
where children pick them in handfuls
ignoring those who say they are weeds

October Nights

pink orange
scarves of clouds
wrap up the world

for the first time
it is as if we have reached
the exact corner of earth

where the sky bends around us
like the smooth curve
of a carved pumpkin

and we are inside
emitting its glow

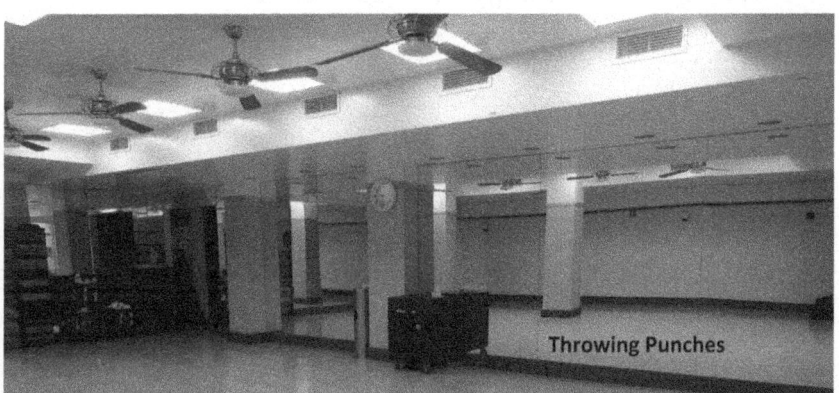

Throwing Punches

During a jab/cross/uppercut combo I pound my fists towards an invisible enemy, wanting nothing more than to add a roundhouse kick to the jab to take the air off guard, ripping muscles to grow them back stronger

if the heart is a muscle, then you are my personal trainer, tearing fibers enclosing my strength, and here I am cradling it, thinking it an injury, that little scars are being chipped into my perfect red construction paper heart, but

no, it thrives on the tear, bring it on, says my heart, rip me, shred me, I am not paper, I am muscle, and through the drips that look like cries, I am getting stronger, the floor may appear hard, but it is my support, I may look spent, but I am just getting started

Throwing Punches

I sit on the hardwood gym floor resined in sweat
and inhale the scent of rubber shoes as I lean toward
my own sole, pull back the toes, allow the hamstring
to stretch until it burns, breathe in, tightens
breathe out, relaxes

the instructor walks in, a tattoo crawls across on her back
of what appears to be a paisley quilt
wrapping her shoulders like a shawl
not as badass as her manicured fauxhawk

I stand up, adjust my ballet pink tank top and black pants
with matching pink stripe, tighten my massive curly ponytail
lock my arms in front of my face to guard
prepare to kick the crap out of the mirror for staring back

my sneakers bob and weave
jumping in and out of sweat puddles
curls escape their holder in a prison break
skin becomes an oil slick of pavement during a storm

during a jab, cross, upper cut combo
I sneak a peek at the crowd behind me
some with water bottles upside down
not caring if water was going in their mouth or down their neck
just wanting the cold
others gasp against a pole, but some

some are like me
eyes focused on reflections
pounding fists against oxygen
finding fault in the invisible enemy confronting us
wanting nothing more than to add a roundhouse kick
to the jab to take the air off guard
ripping muscles to grow them back stronger

if the heart is a muscle, then you are my personal trainer
tearing the fibers enclosing my strength
week after week after bloody damn week
and here I am cradling it, thinking it an injury
that little scars are being chipped into the perfect
red construction paper heart with kid safe scissors, but

no, it thrives on the tear, bring it on, says my heart
rip me, shred me, I am no paper, I am muscle
and through the drips that look like cries I am getting stronger
the floor may appear hard, but it is my support
I may look spent, but I am just getting started

This Moment

Umbrellas are up
but it's not raining
bubbled circles of black
skim the surface of grease-slicked pavement
we slip through foggy curtains
inhaling clouds

on cold pulsing streets
liquid neon replaces blood
pumping through plastic veins
we glow in the dark

stars draw swords
in battle with granite buildings
the moon peeks in an aisle of sky

we walk with the weight of happy endings
trailing like cans at our heels

a blank newspaper wraps around a leg
we pause to read the headline
it blinks then whispers
go

What Was Lost

Words spilled in blue swirls
that leapt at each jolt of the train
I curved my pages inward
to avoid uninvited eyes
as I raced to fill the faded lines

I became so involved in those scraps of paper
that when they called my stop
I almost missed it

& jumped from my seat
gathering loose sheets
like a child collecting leaves

I raced through silver sliding doors
turning back only once to see
what was lost—

a poem

detached from me

flapping
  loosely
          to the ground

a silent remnant of myself

released, unguarded
free

Kerri Davidson is a poet, memoirist, and screenwriter based in New York City. Her poem, "This Moment" won the 2017 Heart Poetry Award and was published, along with "Beginnings", which received an honorable mention, in the Heart 12 Anthology. Portions of her memoir have been published in *Chicken Soup for the Soul: Power of the Positive*, *Hope Whispers*, and *Skirt! Magazine*. She co-wrote the screenplay for the award-winning short film, *Finding You*, which was named one of the Top Ten Films in the Film Lab's 72 Hour Shootout competition and was screened at the Time Warner Center in New York City and at the Japanese American National Museum in Los Angeles. Kerri has read excerpts of her memoir and poetry at various New York City venues. In her free time, she loves to dance. Follow her on Instagram @thedustdancing and check out her website: www.kerridavidson.com.

www.ingramcontent.com/pod-product-compliance
Lightning Source LLC
LaVergne TN
LVHW041507070426
835507LV00012B/1382